CocoWyo

OCEAN SCENE
BOLD - EASY COLORING BOOK

Immerse yourself in the tranquil beauty of our exquisite illustrations of oceanic creatures. Each page offers a peaceful escape, allowing you to alleviate stress and find relaxation as you bring these serene underwater scenes to life with your colors.

PUBLISHED IN 2024 BY COCO WYO PUBLISHING

COLOR YOURSELF HAPPY!

In today's demanding world, managing our mental health is vital. Recent years have taken a toll on us, and that's why immersing ourselves in art has become an essential part of our self-care routine, bringing joy and inner peace.

 ## PAPER CHOICE

We choose standard-quality paper for affordability due to the limited paper options on Amazon. You can prevent bleeding that may occur with certain pens or markers by placing a blank sheet of thicker paper behind the page you're coloring. We appreciate your understanding of our paper selection.

 ## SHARE YOUR ARTWORKS

Since launching our Adult Coloring Books on Amazon, we've seen countless pages come to life by creative colorists like you. When you leave feedback, feel free to share pictures and celebrate your unique creations. We are excited to see your masterpieces! ☺

CONNECT WITH US

For any concerns, please feel free to contact us at **support@cocowyo.com**

(@cocowyocoloring)

50+ FREE DIGITAL COLORING PAGES!

Thank you for choosing our book!
Visit the "Coco Wyo Coloring Community" Facebook group
to download them now!

Share your fabulous finished artwork with us!
Join our Facebook group to let your creativity shine.
Scan the QR code to join the group:

 @cocowyocoloring   Coco Wyo Coloring Books

THIS BOOK
BELONGS TO

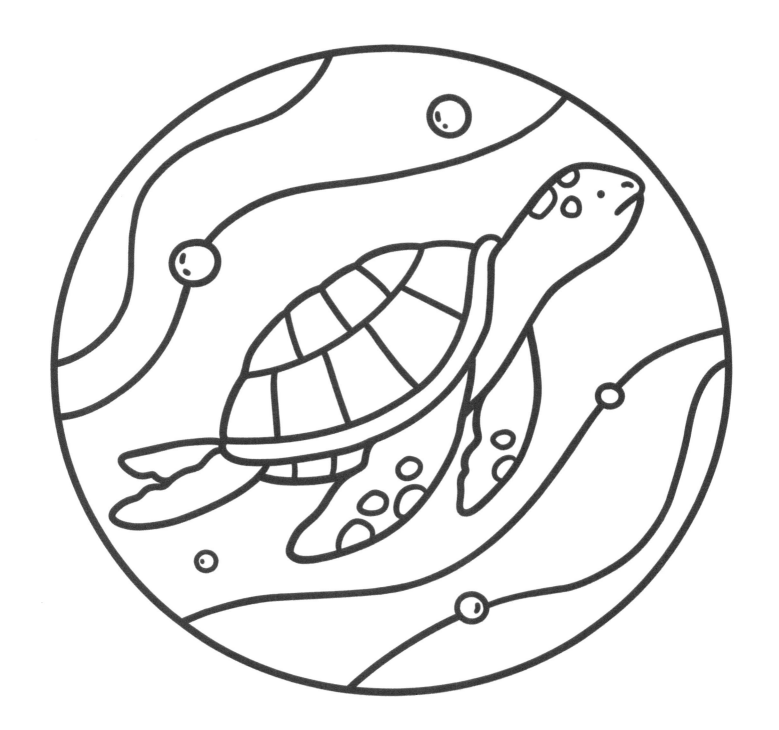

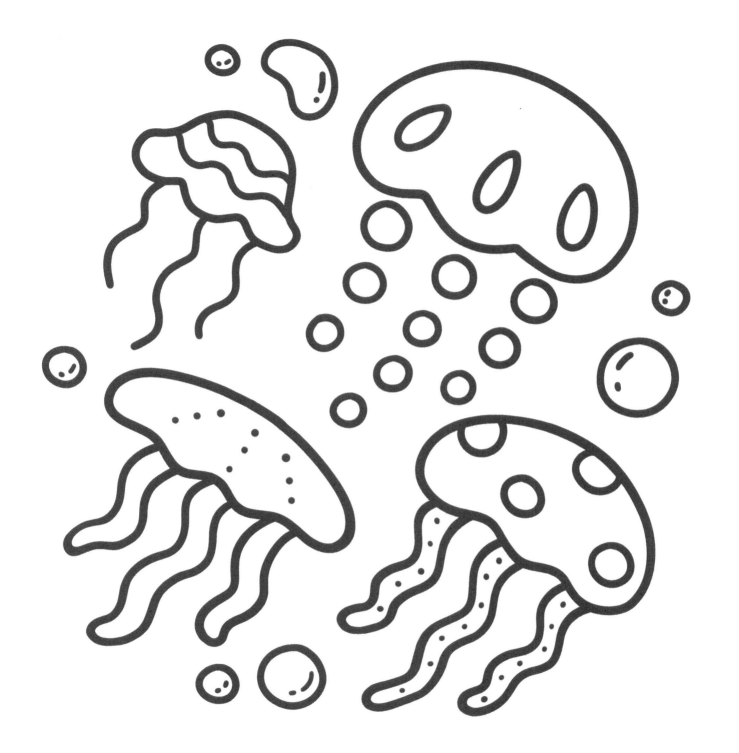

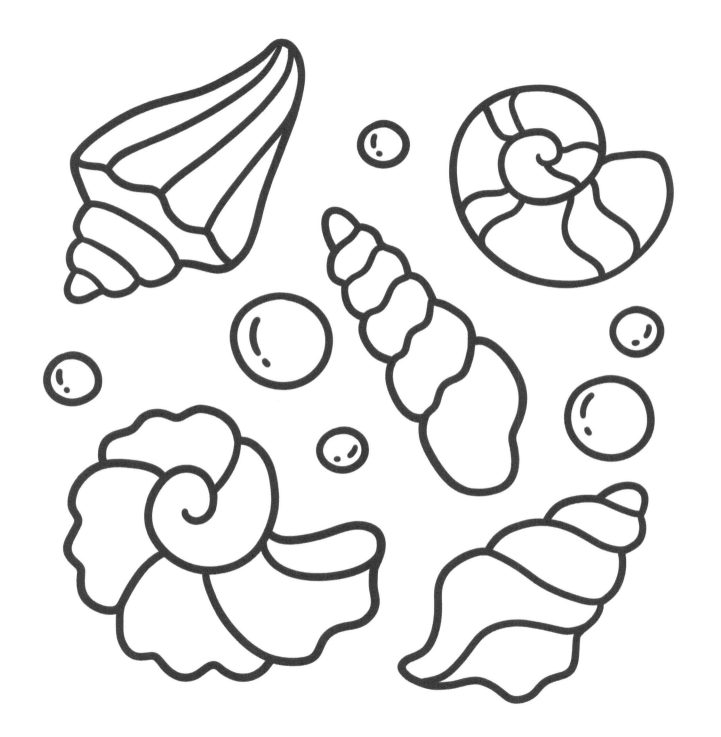

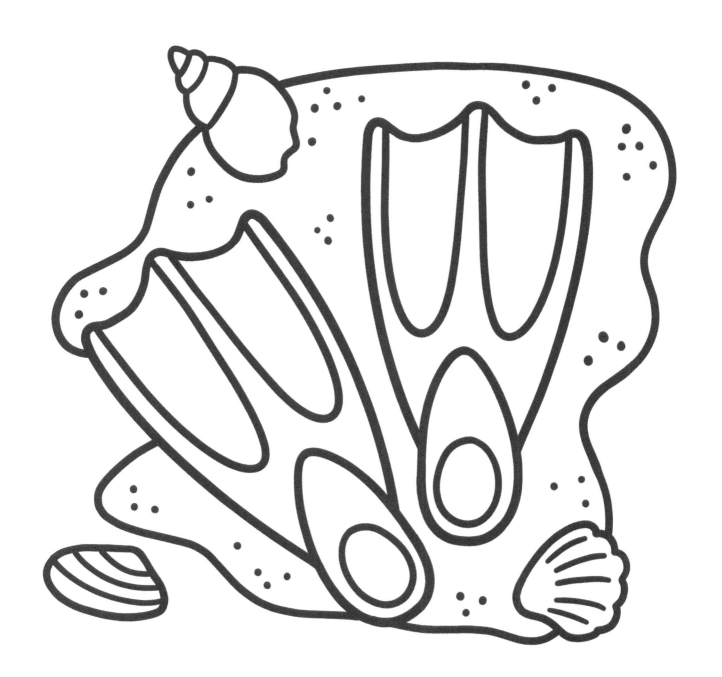

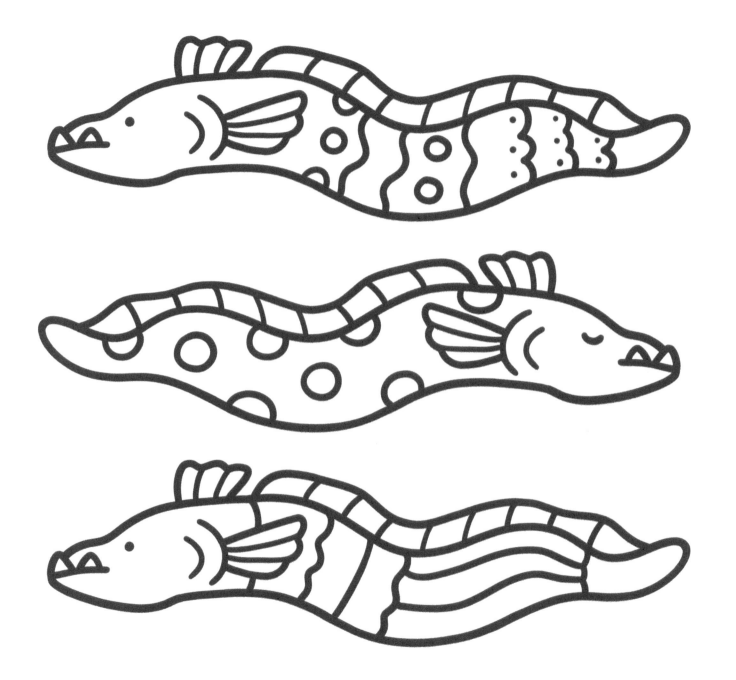